ISAAC ASIMOV'S
LIBRARY OF THE UNIVERSE

HOW WAS THE UNIVERSE BORN?

by Isaac Asimov

DELL YEARLING NONFICTION

Published by
Dell Publishing
a division of
Bantam Doubleday Dell Publishing Group, Inc.
666 Fifth Avenue
New York, New York 10103

This edition was first published in the United States and Canada in 1989
by Gareth Stevens, Inc.

Technical advisers and consulting editors: Fran Millhouser, Greg Walz-Chojnacki,
and Francis Reddy

ISBN: 0-440-40442-8

Reprinted by arrangement with Gareth Stevens, Inc.

Printed in the United States of America
August 1991

10 9 8 7 6 5 4 3 2 1

CONTENTS

Nowadays, we have seen planets up close, all the way to distant Neptune. We have mapped Venus through its clouds. We have seen the rings around Neptune and the ice volcanoes on Triton, one of Neptune's moons. We have put spacecraft with measuring devices on the surfaces of Mars and Venus. Human beings have even walked on our Moon!

But the greatest drama of all is to try to understand the Universe as a whole. We can only begin to try to grasp its vastness and to study all the strange things we find in it. Some of these things — quasars, pulsars, and black holes — we didn't even dream of until the last few decades. We have sent the robot probe COBE (Cosmic Background Explorer) on a mission to study the fading glow of the Big Bang, the explosion which began the Universe.

So let's learn a bit about the amazing story of our Universe!

Isaac Asimov

Above: According to ancient Greek myths, the god Helios drove the chariot that carries the Sun across the sky.

Left: Nut, a sky goddess of ancient Egypt.

Right: The stars of summer gleam like jewels on the dome of the night sky.

Primitive Ideas

Long ago, human beings could only suppose that the Universe was what it looked like to them.

The Earth? It seemed to be no more than a round patch of flat ground, not very big. The sky? It seemed to be a solid dome that came down to meet the ground all around, at places not far off. The Sun? It traveled across the sky to give us light and warmth. The sky was blue when the Sun was present, but turned black when it set. In the night sky, there were many, many specks of light — stars — in the dome of the sky. The Moon, which went through a change of shape every month, moved among the stars. A few stars were brighter than the others, and they also moved.

Where Is Earth?

The ancient Greeks said that Earth was a large sphere and thought it was at the center of the Universe. They thought that the Moon circled around the Earth. Outside the Moon's orbit circled Mercury, Venus, the Sun, Mars, Jupiter, and Saturn. Outside the orbits of all these bodies were the sky and the stars.

In 1543, Copernicus (pronounced co-PER-nic-us), a Polish astronomer (1473-1543), showed that the planets, including the Earth, circled the Sun in orbits, and that beyond the planets were the stars. Later, Edmund Halley, an English astronomer (1656-1742) noted for his work on comets, found out that the stars moved, too.

Left: Nicolaus Copernicus — the Polish philosopher, doctor, and astronomer who showed that the planets circle the Sun.

Lower left: the Copernican system. The Sun lies in the center and Earth circles around it.

Below: Star trails in a time-exposure photo of the night sky. From where we stand on Earth, the Sun, Moon, planets, and stars all seem to wheel across the sky — small wonder people once thought Earth was the center of the Universe!

Island Universes

In 1785, William Herschel (HER-shell) showed that Earth is in a large collection of stars shaped like a lens. We call this collection the Milky Way Galaxy. This is our Galaxy, and it is 100,000 light-years across. Each light-year is almost six trillion miles (9.5 trillion km) long.

There are other galaxies as well. They look like cloudy patches in the sky, but they are really other galaxies very far away. The closest large galaxy is the Andromeda galaxy, which is over two million light-years away. Many other galaxies are scattered through space. There might be a hundred billion in all!

The German-born English astronomer William Herschel, discoverer of the planet Uranus. He designed the best telescopes of his time.

If we could view our Milky Way from the outside, it would look like the great galaxy in Andromeda, seen here without the aid of a telescope.

Right: Through a telescope, ragged dust clouds appear around the Andromeda galaxy's core. Over two million light-years away, it's the closest galaxy that resembles our own spiral, the Milky Way.

The Red Shift

In 1842, Christian Doppler explained why anything noisy sounds more shrill when it comes toward you, and sounds deeper when it goes away from you. A similar kind of change, or shift, happens with light.

Austrian scientist
Christian Doppler.

Every star sends out light waves. The light appears bluer if the star is coming toward us, and redder if it is moving away. In the 1920s, astronomers found that most galaxies show a "red shift." This means that they are moving away from our Galaxy. The farther away they are, the faster they move away from us. The farthest galaxies are moving away at thousands of miles a second!

When light from a star or galaxy is spread out into a rainbow of color, dark lines show up where light has been absorbed by the atoms of that star or galaxy. The lines in the light of distant galaxies are shifted toward ever redder light as they move farther away from us.

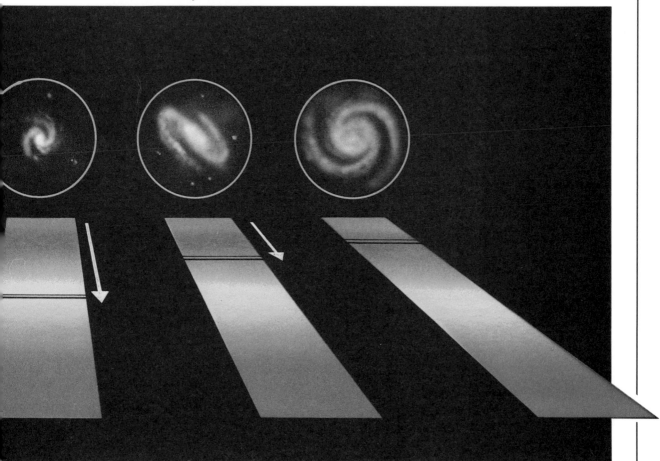

The Outer Limits

The most distant galaxies we can see are hundreds of millions of light-years away. In the 1950s, astronomers discovered certain galaxies that sent out radio waves. These galaxies were studied carefully, and the light waves they sent out looked very strange. In 1963, astronomers found that this was because the light waves were very stretched out.

Galaxies like this are called quasars. Quasars had the largest red shifts known, so they must be very far away. Even the closest quasars are a billion light-years away. One quasar discovered recently is 12 billion light-years away! So when we look at quasars, we are looking back into a time before our Sun was born!

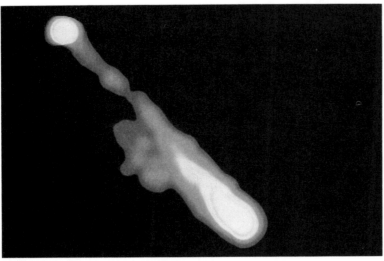

Radio telescopes created this image of a huge gas jet erupting from quasar 3C 273. The jet is a million light-years long!

Right: Appearances can be deceiving. A bridge of gas seems to connect a quasar (top) to a much closer galaxy (below). Astronomers believe that such connections are optical illusions. Colors are added to the picture to bring out faint details.

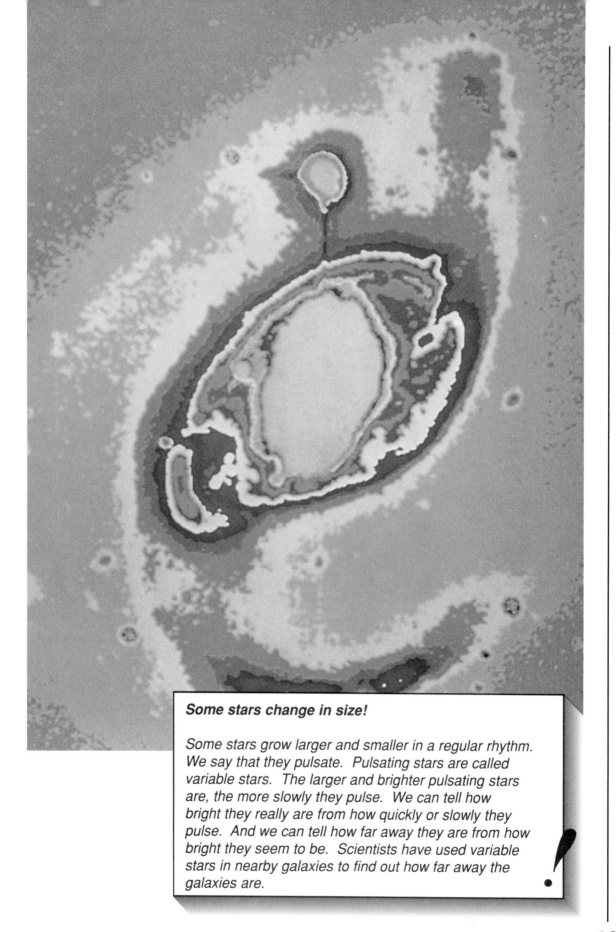

Some stars change in size!

Some stars grow larger and smaller in a regular rhythm. We say that they pulsate. Pulsating stars are called variable stars. The larger and brighter pulsating stars are, the more slowly they pulse. We can tell how bright they really are from how quickly or slowly they pulse. And we can tell how far away they are from how bright they seem to be. Scientists have used variable stars in nearby galaxies to find out how far away the galaxies are.

The Universe — It's a Big Place!

The known planets orbit the Sun in a region only about seven billion miles (11 billion km) in diameter. That's just a little over a thousandth of a light-year. The nearest star is 4.2 light-years away. That's thousands of times as far away as the farthest planet in our Solar system.

The farthest stars in our Galaxy are 100,000 light-years away. The Andromeda galaxy is over two million light-years away,

We think of Earth as quite big, but this painting puts us in our place! From left to right, we see that Earth is just one of nine worlds orbiting the Sun. Our Sun itself is just one of 200 billion stars in the Milky Way Galaxy. The Milky Way is but one of many galaxies in our cluster, and one of <u>billions</u> of galaxies in the Universe.

but it's our next-door neighbor. The farthest known quasar is about 12 billion light-years away.

In all the Universe, there are about 100 billion galaxies. And each galaxy contains about 100 billion stars.

Imagine how small our own Earth is in comparison!

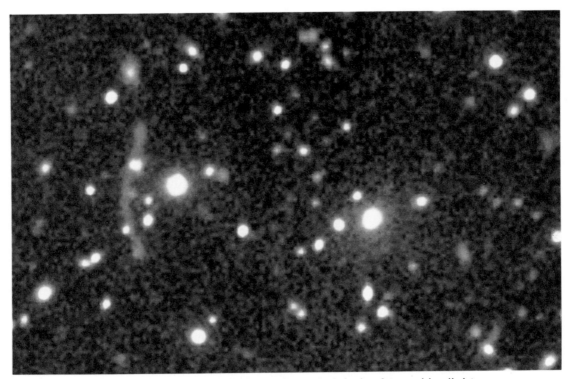

A galaxy cluster. The glowing arcs in this picture might be formed by light pulled off course by a tremendous but unidentified source of gravity. No one knows for sure.

The Expanding Universe

Why are all the galaxies moving away from us? Why should the galaxies farthest away from us move away the fastest? What's so special about us?

The answer is that it isn't us at all! Galaxies exist in groups called clusters. Every cluster moves away from every other cluster. No matter what cluster we might live in, the others would be moving away from us. The Universe is always expanding — growing larger. The space between galaxies is getting bigger. But scientists didn't know this until 1929.

Why is the Universe like soap bubbles?

Throughout the Universe, galaxies seem to form lines and even curves. They enclose large spaces in which there seems to be very little matter. If we could look at the Universe from a great distance and see it all at once, we would think it looked like soap bubbles. Galaxies would be like the soap film making up the bubbles. The bubbles themselves would be empty and come in different sizes. Astronomers still don't know why the galaxies were formed in this way.

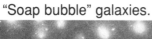

"Soap bubble" galaxies.

The Big Bang

The Universe is expanding as time goes on.
But suppose we look backward in time.

As we go farther and farther back in time, the
galaxies move closer and closer together. If we
went back in time far enough, all the galaxies
would crunch together into a small space.

That was the way it was in the beginning. The
whole thing must have exploded in a "Big Bang."
The Universe is still expanding as a result of that
Big Bang. If we measure how fast the Universe is
expanding and how long it must have taken to
reach its present size, we know that the Big Bang
happened 15 to 20 billion years ago.

Okay — but what came __before__ the Big Bang?

*As scientists try to figure out the history of the
Universe, they reach a point where the laws of
science don't seem to work. They can only describe
the Universe a fraction of a second after the Big Bang.
But what existed __before__ the birth of the Universe?
Maybe the cosmos was born from __nothing__. But
no one can really say!*

Imagine that galaxies are like the raisins in raisin bread dough. The raisins start off fairly close together (top). If you could stand on any one of them as the dough expands (bottom), all the other raisins would appear to be moving away from you. As space expands, all the galaxies appear to be moving away from us.

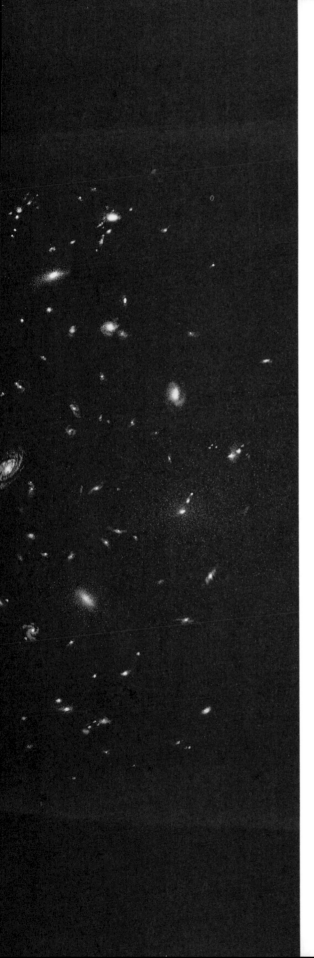

Whispers of the Big Bang

At the time of the Big Bang, all the matter and energy of the Universe was squeezed into one tiny spot! It must have been very hot — trillions of degrees.

But as the Universe expanded, it cooled off. There are still hot spots, like the stars, but overall, the Universe has become much cooler. The light waves of the vast flash of the Big Bang stretched and grew longer as the Universe cooled. Today, they are very long radio waves.

In 1965, those radio waves were detected. Scientists could hear the last faint whisper of the Big Bang of long ago.

This painting shows the history of our expanding Universe. The bright spot on the left represents the Big Bang itself. As you look further to the right, subatomic particles form, then atoms of matter. Next, gas clumps together to form galaxies. Then, within those galaxies, gas further clumps to make stars and planets.

The Early Universe

Light travels at a speed of 186,000 miles (300,000 km) a second. If a star is 10 light-years from us, its light takes 10 years to reach us.

Since the Andromeda galaxy is over two million light-years from us, its light takes over two million years to reach us! This means that the farther out in <u>space</u> we look, the farther back in <u>time</u> we see!

Light from the most distant known quasar takes about 12 billion years to reach us. Since the Big Bang happened about 15 to 20 billion years ago, we see distant quasars as they looked when the Universe was quite young. In 1988, astronomers announced that they had found objects 17 billion light-years away. They were galaxies being formed when the Universe was still younger. We can't see much farther than that!

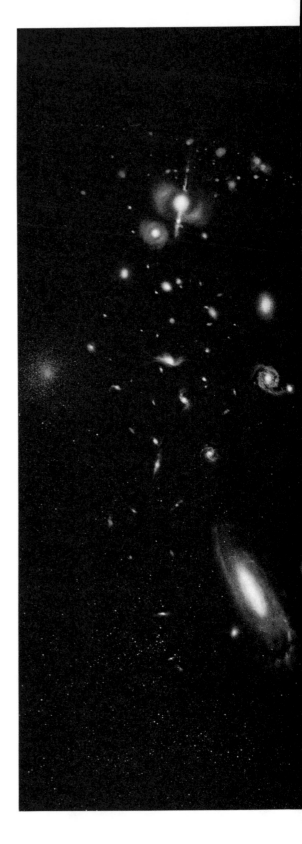

How far is far? The light from our Sun (shown to the upper right of Earth) takes just eight minutes to reach us. Light from the nearest star, Alpha Centauri (the bluish speck shown below Earth), takes 4.2 years. The light we see from the great galaxy in Andromeda (the spiral shown at lower left) left 2.3 million years ago. And light from the farthest known quasars (upper left) set out 12 billion to 15 billion years ago.

How the Universe Changes

Stars stay hot because of nuclear changes in their centers. As a star center grows hotter, the star expands. Eventually, the star explodes and collapses.

When a very large star explodes, it becomes a supernova. Supernovas spread their material through space. In the Big Bang, only the simplest atoms, hydrogen and helium, were formed, but supernovas spread more complex atoms outward.

Our Sun formed from a cloud with these more complex atoms. Almost all the atoms of Earth — and in ourselves — were formed in stars that exploded as supernovas long ago.

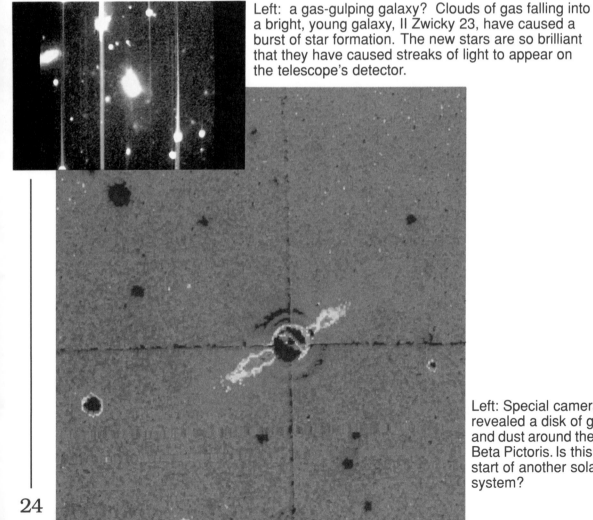

Left: a gas-gulping galaxy? Clouds of gas falling into a bright, young galaxy, II Zwicky 23, have caused a burst of star formation. The new stars are so brilliant that they have caused streaks of light to appear on the telescope's detector.

Left: Special cameras revealed a disk of gas and dust around the star Beta Pictoris. Is this the start of another solar system?

Above: Stars can explode with incredible violence, becoming so bright that they outshine a whole galaxy of normal stars. Supernovas also spread complex elements into space, and the force of the explosions helps stars begin to form.

Left: Galaxy NGC 5128 before (top) and after (bottom) it had a supernova.

A crab in the sky!

In 1054, a supernova only about 5,000 light-years away appeared in the sky. It was brighter than the planet Venus, but a year or so later, it faded away. But what is left of it can still be seen as a small, oddly shaped cloudy patch right where the supernova was. It is a cloud of debris left by the explosion. It's called the Crab Nebula because of its shape. The Crab Nebula has been expanding for almost 1,000 years after the explosion. In its center, there is a tiny neutron star, all that is left of the original giant star that exploded. ●

What Will Happen to the Universe?

When a supernova explodes, what is left of it can collapse into a tiny object with gravity so strong that everything falls in, but nothing comes out. This object is called a black hole. There might be a black hole in the center of every galaxy.

The Universe may expand forever, or its own gravity might someday slow its expansion, and even stop it. It might then fall back together in a Big Crunch. And maybe a new Universe will form in a new Big Bang.

Maybe there was a Big Crunch, or even many Big Crunches, before the Big Bang that formed our Universe. We don't know if there ever was. We're still trying to understand the Big Bang that created the present Universe. That's a big enough puzzle for now!

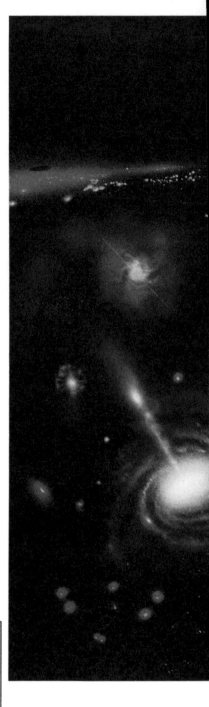

Mini-stars with maxi-mass

When a star explodes and collapses, it becomes incredibly smaller than you might ever expect. It's like breaking up Ping-Pong balls and packing their pieces. Some stars collapse into white dwarf stars. White dwarfs can be smaller than Earth, but they can hold the same amount of matter as the Sun! Even smaller stars, called neutron stars, are formed when very large stars collapse. Neutron stars can be as massive as our Sun, but they might be only a few miles in diameter!

Someday in the very distant future, perhaps the Universe will stop expanding and begin contracting. Everything in the cosmos would fall into an enormous black hole (top of painting) — and perhaps create another Big Bang!

Fact File: Distance and Size in the Universe

We know the Universe is a big place. But just how big is it?

We can talk about the great distances and sizes that exist in the Universe. But maybe the best way to get an idea about just how big those distances and sizes really are is to compare them to distances and sizes we know about and use here on Earth.

Imagine that we could reduce the cosmos to a size we can manage. First let's imagine that we could make the Sun the size of a soccer ball. Then let's shrink the Universe even further, so we could put the entire Solar system in a coffee cup. And finally, let's shrink the entire known Universe down so that all of our Galaxy, the Milky Way, would be no wider than a long-playing record!

Even after reducing the Universe this much, we might be surprised at how far apart everything in the cosmos still seems. We can use the illustration above and the charts on page 29 to get an idea of how big and how far everything is out there — and how much space there is in space.

The Sun as a Soccer Ball

What if the Sun was...	Then Earth (our home planet) could be...	And Jupiter (the Solar system's biggest planet) would be...	And Pluto (our Solar system's tiniest known planet) could be...	And Alpha Centauri (the nearest star in our Galaxy) would be...
...a soccer ball about 8 3/4 inches (22 cm) wide?	...a pebble less than 1/10 inch (1/4 cm) wide, and about 78 1/2 feet (24 m) from our soccer-ball Sun.	...a bit bigger than a ball bearing 7/8 inch (2.2 cm) wide.	...a pebble tinier even than Earth, and over 1/2 mile (0.8 km) from our soccer-ball Sun.	...nearly 4 miles (6.4 km) from the soccer-ball Sun at the center of our Solar system.

The Solar System in a Cup

And what if our Solar system was...	Then the Milky Way (our Galaxy) would be...
...small enough to fit in a coffee cup?	...as wide as North America — about 3,000 miles (4,800 km) across!

The Milky Way as a Long-playing Record!

And what if the Milky Way (our Galaxy) was...	Then the Andromeda Galaxy (the galaxy "next door") would be...	And the farthest-known quasars would be...
...a long-playing record about 1 foot (30 cm) wide?	...23 feet (7 m) away from the Milky Way.	...more than 32 miles (51 km) away from the Milky Way!

As big as we think Earth is, it is only a tiny speck in our vast Universe!

More Books About the Universe

Here are more books that contain information about the Universe. If you are interested in them, check your library or bookstore.

Nightwatch: An Equinox Guide to Viewing the Universe. Dickinson (Camden)
Our Milky Way and Other Galaxies. Asimov (Gareth Stevens)
Quasars, Pulsars, and Black Holes. Asimov (Gareth Stevens)
Space & Beyond. Montgomery (Bantam)
The Stars: From Birth to Black Hole. Darling (Dillon)
Universe. Zim (Morrow)
Universe: Past, Present & Future. Darling (Dillon)

Places to Visit

You can explore many places in the Universe without leaving Earth. Here are some museums and centers where you can find a variety of space exhibits.

National Museum of Science and Technology
Ottawa, Ontario

Touch the Universe
Manitoba Planetarium
Winnipeg, Manitoba

H. R. MacMillan Planetarium
Vancouver, British Columbia

Henry Crown Space Center
Museum of Science and Industry
Chicago, Illinois

Kansas Cosmosphere and Space Center
Hutchinson, Kansas

American Museum — Hayden Planetarium
New York, New York

Science North Solar Observatory
Sudbury, Ontario

McDonald Observatory
Austin, Texas

For More Information About the Universe

Here are some places you can write to for more information about the Universe. Be sure to tell them exactly what you want to know about or see. Remember to include your age, full name, and address.

For information about astronomy:
NASA Kennedy Space Center
Educational Services Office
Kennedy Space Center, Florida 32899

Space Communications Branch
Ministry of State for Science and Technology
240 Sparks Street, C. D. Howe Building
Ottawa, Ontario K1A 1A1, Canada

For photographs of stars and galaxies:
Caltech Bookstore
California Institute of Technology
Mail Code 1-51
Pasadena, California 91125

For catalogs of slides, posters, sky maps, and other astronomy material:
AstroMedia Order Department
21027 Crossroads Circle
Waukesha, Wisconsin 53187

National Museum of Science and Technology
Astronomy Division
2380 Lancaster Road
Ottawa, Ontario K1A 0M8, Canada

Sky Publishing Corporation
49 Bay State Road
Cambridge, Massachusetts 02238-1290

Glossary

Andromeda galaxy: the closest spiral galaxy to our own — over two million light-years away.

atoms: the smallest particles of elements that can exist. They are the source of nuclear energy when joined together or split apart.

the Big Bang: a gigantic explosion that many scientists believe created our Universe.

billion: in North America — and in this book — the number represented by 1 followed by nine zeroes — 1,000,000,000. In some places, such as the United Kingdom (Britain), this number is called "a thousand million." In these places, one billion would then be represented by 1 followed by 12 zeroes — 1,000,000,000,000: a million million, a number known as a trillion in North America.

black hole: an object in space caused by the explosion and collapse of a star. This object is so tightly packed that not even light can escape the force of its gravity.

Copernicus, Nicolaus: the first modern scholar to suggest, in 1543, that the Sun was at the center of the Universe, with the planets orbiting around it.

Doppler, Christian: the Austrian scientist who, in 1842, showed why noise sounds more shrill when coming toward you, but sounds deeper when moving away from you. Light waves act in a similar way. They are shorter — and appear blue — when they are coming toward you, and become longer — and appear red — when moving away. (See also **red shift**.)

galaxy: any of the billions of large groupings of stars, gas, and dust that exist in the Universe. Our Galaxy is known as the Milky Way Galaxy.

Herschel, William: the German astronomer who, in 1785, showed that the visible stars are all part of a vast collection of stars. He said that our Sun was part of this collection, which today we know as the Milky Way Galaxy.

light-year: the distance that light travels in one year — nearly six trillion miles (9.6 trillion km).

nebula: a cloud of dust and gas in space. Some large nebulas, or nebulae, are the birthplaces of stars. Other nebulae are the debris of dying stars.

neutron stars: very small stars formed when large stars collapse, but which keep much of their very great mass.

optical illusion: something perceived by the eye, a camera, or a telescope that is not what it appears to be. For example, the appearance of a "bridge" of gases from a quasar to a galaxy may be false, a trick played on the "eye" of the telescope — an optical illusion.

quasars: the most distant galaxies in the Universe. They are billions of light-years away from Earth.

radio waves: electromagnetic waves that can be detected by radio receiving equipment.

red shift: the apparent reddening of light given off by an object moving away from us (see **Doppler, Christian**). The greater the red shift of light from a distant galaxy, the faster that galaxy is moving away from us.

sphere: a globelike body. The ancient Greeks believed that Earth was a large sphere at the center of the Universe.

supernova: the result of a huge star exploding. When a supernova occurs, material from the star is spread through space.

Universe: everything that we know exists and believe may exist.

variable stars: stars whose brightness changes. Some variable stars change brightness very regularly. Others are unpredictable.

Index

The publishers wish to thank the following for permission to reproduce copyright material: front cover, pp. 17, 19 (both), © Julian Baum, 1988; p. 4 (upper), © Sally Bensusen, 1988; pp. 4 (lower), 8 (upper), 10 (upper), photographs courtesy of Julian Baum; p. 5, © Frank Zullo, 1987; p. 6 (upper), AIP Niels Bohr Library; p. 6 (lower), Mary Evans Picture Library; p. 7, © Anglo-Australian Telescope Board, David Malin, 1980; p. 8 (lower), © George East, 1978; pp. 9, 13, 16, 24 (upper), 25 (lower), National Optical Astronomy Observatories; pp. 10-11, 14-15, © Brian Sullivan, 1988; p. 12, Science Photo Library; pp. 20-21, 22-23, © Paternostro / Schaller, 1988; p. 24 (lower), Jet Propulsion Laboratory; pp. 25 (upper), 26-27, © Mark Paternostro, 1988; pp. 28-29, © Larry Ortiz, 1988.